CPS-Morrill ES

3245710500140 2

Hollihan, Kerrie Logan                    394.25 HOL
Carnival in Latin America (bilingual)

 **W9-BWF-466**

**DATE DUE**

4.25
HOL

Hollihan, Kerrie Logan
Carnival in Latin America
(bilingual)

$15.95
BC#32457105001402

| DATE DUE | BORROWER'S NAME |
|---|---|
| | |
| | |
| | |

394.25          BC#32457105001402 $15.95
HOL
Hollihan, Kerrie Logan
Carnival in Latin America
(bilingual)

*Morrill ES*
*Chicago Public Schools*
*6011 S Rockwell St.*
*Chicago, IL  60629*

Latin American Celebrations
and Festivals

# Carnival in Latin America
# Carnaval en Latinoamérica

**Kerrie Logan Hollihan**

**Traducción al español:
Ma. Pilar Sanz**

**PowerKiDS** press & **Editorial Buenas Letras**™
New York

*For Brandon, who has fond memories of Mardi Gras*

Published in 2010 by The Rosen Publishing Group, Inc.
29 East 21st Street, New York, NY 10010

Copyright © 2010 by The Rosen Publishing Group, Inc.

All rights reserved. No part of this book may be reproduced in any form without permission in writing from the publisher, except by a reviewer.

First Edition

Editor: Nicole Pristash
Book Design: Greg Tucker
Photo Researcher: Jessica Gerweck

Photo Credits: Cover Doug Armand/Getty Images; pp. 5, 11 Antonio Scorza/AFP/Getty Images; p. 7 Imagno/Getty Images; p. 9 © Steve Vidler/age fotostock; p. 13 Vanderlei Almeida/AFP/Getty Images; p. 15 © Hughes Hervé/age fotostock; p. 17 © Angelo Cavalli/age fotostock; p. 19 Steve Bly/Getty Images; p. 21 Chris Graythen/Getty Images.

Library of Congress Cataloging-in-Publication Data

Hollihan, Kerrie Logan.
  Carnival in Latin America — Carnaval en Latinoamérica / Kerrie Logan Hollihan. — 1st ed.
    p. cm. — (Latin American celebrations and festivals — Celebraciones y festivales en Latinoamérica)
  Includes index.
  ISBN 978-1-4358-9366-5 (library binding)
  1. Carnival—Latin America—Juvenile literature. 2. Latin America—Social life and customs—Juvenile literature. I. Title. II. Title: Carnaval en Latinoamérica.
  GT4213.5.H65 2010
  394.25098—dc22
                                2009032099

Manufactured in the United States of America

CPSIA Compliance Information: Batch #WW10PK: For Further Information contact Rosen Publishing, New York, New York at 1-800-237-9932

# CONTENTS

1 Carnival!     4

2 Wild Rio     10

3 The Islands Celebrate     16

Glossary     23

Index     24

Web Sites     24

# CONTENIDO

1 ¡Es tiempo de carnaval!     4

2 Fiesta en Río     10

3 Celebración en las islas     16

Glosario     23

Índice     24

Páginas de Internet     24

In January, Latin Americans prepare for carnival (KAHR-nuh-vul), which comes in February or March. During carnival, people **celebrate** life by going to lively parties and colorful parades. The best-known carnival takes place in Brazil. However, other countries celebrate carnival, too.

En enero, Latinoamérica se prepara para la época de carnaval, que viene en febrero y marzo. La gente **celebra** durante carnaval organizando divertidas fiestas y desfiles llenos de color. El carnaval más famoso se celebra en Brasil, pero muchos otros países celebran sus propios carnavales.

Thousands of people travel to Rio de Janeiro, Brazil, to celebrate carnival, shown here.

Miles de personas viajan a Río de Janeiro, Brasil, para celebrar el carnaval que vemos aquí.

Carnival's roots are in many places. It was Christians in Europe, however, who first held wild celebrations before the start of Lent. Lent is the 40 days before Easter when some Christians gave up things that they enjoyed. Many Christians still do this today.

---

El carnaval tiene sus raíces en muchos lugares. Sin embargo, fueron los grupos de cristianos en Europa los primeros en celebrarlo antes del comienzo de la Cuaresma. La Cuaresma es el período de 40 días antes de la fiesta de Pascua. En la Cuaresma los cristianos dejan de hacer algunas cosas que disfrutan.

Many European cities still hold carnival. These people are celebrating in Venice, Italy.
Muchas ciudades europeas organizan carnavales. Estas personas están en Venecia, Italia.

7

This celebration then spread into Latin America, and each country came up with its own **traditions**. In most places, carnival starts on a weekend and stops at midnight on Ash Wednesday, the first day of Lent. The parties often last for weeks.

---

La celebración de la Cuaresma se propagó por Latinoamérica, y cada país creó sus propias **tradiciones**. En la mayoría de estos países, el carnaval comienza en un fin de semana y termina a la media noche del Miércoles de Ceniza, el primer día de la Cuaresma. Con frecuencia la fiestas duran varias semanas.

In the Caribbean, music and dance are important parts of carnival.

En el Caribe, los bailes y la música son partes muy importantes del carnaval.

9

Rio de Janeiro, Brazil, comes alive during carnival. Many Brazilians, young and old, take part in dance groups called samba (SAHM-buh) schools. Samba is a type of music and dance with European and African roots. During carnival, samba schools dance in parades.

---

Río de Janeiro, en Brasil, se transforma durante el carnaval. Muchos brasileños, grandes y pequeños, bailan en escuelas de samba. La samba es un tipo de baile que tiene raíces en Europa y África. Durante el carnaval, las escuelas de samba participan en los desfiles.

Samba schools often dance alongside wild floats, such as this dragon fl...

Las escuelas de samba bailan junto a grandes carros alegóricos, como este dragon.

Berço do sa

Rio's visitors crowd the sidewalks during carnival. Parade marchers walk and dance to wild beats. At night, partygoers visit masked balls. They dress up as superheroes, princesses, devils, and birds. **Costumes** are full of feathers, beads, shells, and bones.

---

Los visitantes al Carnaval de Río llenan las calles durante el carnaval. Quienes participan en el desfile bailan y cantan alegremente. Por la noche, la gente va a fiestas de máscaras. Muchas personas se disfrazan de superhéroes, princesas, diablos y aves. Los **disfraces** se decoran con plumas, conchas y huesos.

Here you can see a group of dancers dressed up as birds during a parade in Rio.

Aquí vemos a un grupo de bailarines vestidos como pájaros en el Carnaval de Río.

In Mexico, seaside cities, such as Mazatlán and Veracruz, host big parties. Children make *cascarones* (kas-kah-ROH-nays), or eggshells filled with **confetti**. Children break them for good luck. On the streets, people laugh at clowns and jugglers. Fireworks light up the sky.

En México, las ciudades costeras, como Mazatlán y Veracruz, organizan grandes fiestas. Los chicos y chicas hacen rellenan cascarones de huevos con **confeti**. Luego los rompen para la buena suerte. En las calles, la gente ríe con payasos y malabaristas. Los fuegos artificiales iluminan la noche.

These are Chinelo dancers. Chinelo is a Mexican dance that is often seen during carnival.

Estos son bailarines Chinelos. El chinelo es un tipo de baile que se ve durante el carnaval.

On the islands of Trinidad and Tobago, in the Caribbean, people form teams called bands. The bands' members wear costumes, and they dance together through the streets. They dance to calypso (kuh-LIP-soh) music, during which drummers pound on steel pans.

---

En las islas de Trinidad y Tobago en el Caribe, la gente forma bandas. Cada banda baila por las calles y usa un disfraz diferente. Estas bandas tocan y bailan calipso. En la música calipso se usan tambores hechos de metal.

Bands in Trinidad and Tobago often wear fun, colorful costumes to dance in the street.

Las bandas en Trinidad y Tobago se visten con colores divertidos para bailar por la calle.

During carnival, the children of Trinidad and Tobago form bands of their own. Girls and boys dress in shiny costumes that look like butterflies, flowers, knights on horses, and even jellyfish. Some costumes are so big that they must be rolled on wheels as the children walk!

---

Los chicos y chicas de Trinidad y Tobago forman sus propias bandas durante el carnaval. Estos chicos usan disfraces brillantes de mariposas, flores, caballeros medievales, caballos y hasta medusas. Algunos disfraces son tan grandes que necesitan ir en ruedas mientras los chicos caminan.

Carnival may seem like a big party for adults, but children have a lot of fun, too!

El carnaval no sólo es una fiesta para los adultos. Los chicos también se divierten.

Some Americans celebrate during carnival, too. In New Orleans, Louisiana, the celebration is called Mardi Gras (MAHR-dee GRAH). Parades with flashy floats crowd the streets. Costumed riders throw strings of colorful beads to visitors. Rex, the king of Mardi Gras, rules the party.

---

En Estados Unidos también se celebra el carnaval. En Nueva Orleans, Luisiana, la celebración se llama Mardi Gras. Durante el Mardi Gras los carros alegóricos desfilan por las calles. Los participantes en los carros alegóricos se disfrazan y lanzan cuentas multicolores a los visitantes. Rex, el rey de Mardi Gras, encabeza la fiesta.

This is one of the many floats that ride through New Orleans during Mardi Gras.

Este es uno de los carros alegóricos que desfilan en Nueva Orleans, en Mardi Gras.

Carnival is a time to have fun. It is an event that brings joy to people in many countries as they celebrate everything that they enjoy in life. People from Latin America and all over the world come together to celebrate. Carnival welcomes everyone to the party!

---

El carnaval alegra a las personas en muchos países cuando celebran todo lo que disfrutan en sus vidas. La gente en Latinoamérica, y alrededor del mundo, se reúne para celebrarlo. ¡Durante las fiestas de carnaval todos son bienvenidos!

celebrate (SEH-leh-brayt)  To honor an important moment by doing special things.

confetti (kun-FEH-tee)  Very small pieces of colored paper.

costumes (kos-TOOMZ)  Clothes that make a person look like someone or something else.

traditions (truh-DIH-shunz)  Ways of doing things that have been passed down over time.

# Glosario

celebrar  Hacer algo especial para reconocer un momento importante.

confeti (el)  Trozos de papel, muy pequeños, de muchos colores.

disfraces (los)  Ropa que hace que uno se vista como otra persona.

tradiciones (las)  Manera de hacer las cosas que ha sido transmitida a través del paso del tiempo.

# Index

**B**
Brazil, 4, 10

**C**
costumes, 12, 16, 18
countries, 4, 8, 22

**L**
Lent, 6, 8
life, 4, 22

**P**
parades, 4, 10, 20

parties, 4, 8, 14, 20, 22

**S**
samba, 10

**T**
traditions, 8

# Índice

**B**
Brasil, 4, 10

**C**
Cuaresma, 6, 8

**D**
desfiles, 4, 10, 20

disfraces, 12, 16, 18

**F**
fiesta(s), 4, 8, 14, 20, 12, 22

**P**
países, 4, 8, 22

**S**
samba, 10

**T**
tradiciones, 8

**V**
vidas, 22

# Web Sites / Páginas de Internet

Due to the changing nature of Internet links, PowerKids Press has developed an online list of Web sites related to the subject of this book. This site is updated regularly. Please use this link to access the list:
www.powerkidslinks.com/lacf/carnival/